IT'S TIME TO LEARN ABOUT CARDINALS

It's Time to Learn about Cardinals

Walter the Educator

Silent King Books
A WhichHead Entertainment Imprint

Copyright © 2025 by Walter the Educator

All rights reserved. No part of this book may be reproduced in any manner whatsoever without written per- mission except in the case of brief quotations embodied in critical articles and reviews.

First Printing, 2024

Disclaimer

This book is a literary work; the story is not about specific persons, locations, situations, and/or circumstances unless mentioned in a historical context. Any resemblance to real persons, locations, situations, and/or circumstances is coincidental. This book is for entertainment and informational purposes only. The author and publisher offer this information without warranties expressed or implied. No matter the grounds, neither the author nor the publisher will be accountable for any losses, injuries, or other damages caused by the reader's use of this book. The use of this book acknowledges an understanding and acceptance of this disclaimer.

It's Time to Learn about Cardinals is a collectible early learning book by Walter the Educator suitable for all ages belonging to Walter the Educator's Time to Eat Book Series. Collect more books at WaltertheEducator.com

USE THE EXTRA SPACE TO TAKE NOTES AND DOCUMENT YOUR MEMORIES

CARDINALS

High in the trees so bold and bright,

It's Time to Learn about
Cardinals

A flash of red, a lovely sight.

The cardinal sings a tune so sweet,

With whistles clear and notes upbeat.

The male wears feathers crimson red,

A pointed crest upon his head.

The female's brown with hints of hue,

Soft orange beak and golden too.

They sing in winter, loud and strong,

Their cheerful calls a lovely song.

Through frosty winds and snowy days,

Their melody still fills the haze.

They love to perch on branches tall,

And answer when their loved ones call.

A pair for life, they stay so true,

With gentle chirps and feathers new.

It's Time to Learn about
Cardinals

In bushes dense, they build their nests,

A cozy home where eggs can rest.

With twigs and grass, they weave with care,

A hidden spot, so warm in there.

Their favorite foods are seeds and grain,

From sunflower snacks to backyard plain.

They peck at berries, bright and round,

Or feast on bugs upon the ground.

When danger nears, they chirp and fly,

With watchful eyes up in the sky.

A hawk or cat may sneak around,

But cardinals dart without a sound.

In springtime warmth, their babies hatch,

So small and weak, but growing fast.

With open beaks, they chirp for more,

It's Time to Learn about
Cardinals

Till wings are strong enough to soar.

Through all the seasons, near and far,

The cardinal shines just like a star.

A sign of hope, so bright and true,

With songs that bring a peaceful view.

So listen close and you might hear,

A cardinal's tune so bright and clear.

A happy bird, both brave and free,

It's Time to Learn about
Cardinals

A joyful gift for you and me!

ABOUT THE CREATOR

Walter the Educator is one of the pseudonyms for Walter Anderson. Formally educated in Chemistry, Business, and Education, he is an educator, an author, a diverse entrepreneur, and he is the son of a disabled war veteran. "Walter the Educator" shares his time between educating and creating. He holds interests and owns several creative projects that entertain, enlighten, enhance, and educate, hoping to inspire and motivate you. Follow, find new works, and stay up to date with Walter the Educator™ at WaltertheEducator.com

www.ingramcontent.com/pod-product-compliance
Lightning Source LLC
LaVergne TN
LVHW051919060526
838201LV00060B/4083